T0065785

WHEN DARKNESS FALLS

ROLINDA GOLDEN

WESTBOW
PRESS®
A DIVISION OF THOMAS NELSON
& ZONDERVAN

WestBow Press books may be ordered through booksellers or by contacting:

WestBow Press
A Division of Thomas Nelson & Zondervan
1663 Liberty Drive
Bloomington, IN 47403
www.westbowpress.com
844-714-3454

ISBN: 978-1-6642-8375-6 (sc)
ISBN: 978-1-6642-8374-9 (e)

Library of Congress Control Number: 2022921304

Print information available on the last page.

WestBow Press rev. date: 12/08/2022

I dedicate this book to all of you who have suffered, those of you who are suffering now, and those who will suffer in the days to come. I dedicate this book to you who have experienced a great loss: the loss of a loved one, the loss of a longtime companion, the loss of someone special.

I dedicate this to those who are stuck in life, stuck in their feelings, stuck in their minds, stuck in dark places.

My hope and desire is that you read this story with an open mind and receiving heart. If you are stuck, or if you know of anyone who is stuck right now, you both will benefit from my story.

I was in a dark place for years, but by the grace of God and some special people He placed in my life, I came out.

I dedicate this book to my mom, Mother Louise Holland, who loves me unconditionally; without her, there would be no me. I dedicate this book to my three sons Danny Jr., Martell Sr., and Robert Sr. for loving me, holding me up, and keeping me grounded and rooted in love.

I dedicate this book to my sisters Lavita, Faye, Jody, Joyce and Vicky for always being there when I need a shoulder to lean on and an ear to listen.

I dedicate this book to my daughters-in-love Latoya, ShayShay, and Darlene for being the best daughters in the world; there is nothing they wouldn't do for me.

I dedicate this book to my grandchildren for loving, helping and supporting Nana whenever I'm in need.

I dedicate this book to some special friends who never left my side: Ms. Polly, Genise, Dorothy Ann, and Chef Stephanie.

I dedicate this book to two of my nieces, Keda and Shemeka, who are always checking on me. Whenever I'm not feeling my best, it seems like they know because they would text or call me.

I dedicate this book to Mother Emily Riggins for helping me see in me what I needed to see.

Last but not least I dedicate this book to Elaine and Corina of Celebration Church, for opening their arms to me while showing and telling me, "I'm Not Alone.

CONTENTS

When Darkness Falls

When darkness falls, you become blind for you cannot see.
You become a prisoner of darkness who cannot be set free.
You become numb; you cannot move or even think.
You feel like a ship in the ocean about to sink.
You feel like you're underwater trying to hold your breath.
You feel like giving up because you feel there's nothing left.

When darkness falls, you feel all alone.
No one is around to hear your every moan.
You're always sad and blue with heartache and pain—
No sunshine or daylight, just darkness and rain

When darkness falls, you cry all the time.
Feels like you're losing a piece of your mind.
Everything is wrong; nothing is right—
No good days, only horrible nights.

When darkness falls, your spirit falls too.
You're stuck in the dark not knowing what to do.
So you sit in a closet or maybe on the floor,
Thinking to yourself *I can't take this no more*
But something inside says *Don't give up, don't give in,*
This battle in your mind will eventually end.
Just grab my hand and hold on tight.
When darkness falls, just stay in the light.

He Cares

You say no one cares when you're feeling sad and blue.
No one cares about the trials you go through.
No one cares about your heartaches and pain.
No one cares to ask you your name.
No one cares about your tears of sorrow.
No one cares if they see you tomorrow.
No one cares to say I love you.
No one cares about anything you do.
No one cares if you're all alone.
No one cares to visit your home.
No one cares if you're falling all apart.
No one cares about your broken heart.

Well, I'm here to tell you about Jesus Christ.
He cares so much He gave up His life.
He cares when you're feeling sad and blue.
He cares about whatever you're going through.
He cares about your heartaches and pains.
He cares enough, He calls you by name.
He cares about your tears of sorrow.
He cares enough, He will wake you tomorrow.
He cares when you're feeling all alone.
He cares enough, He will visit your home.

So don't ever think that no one cares
When you have someone close who's always there.
Just call on Him in your time of despair.
He's your Lord and Savior and believe me:
He cares.

INTRODUCTION

Stuck

It was July 15, 2016—a beautiful summer morning. We had just returned from a week's vacation in Arizona. My husband, Big Danny, had one more week left of his vacation. I called him Big Danny because we had a son named after him, Danny Jr., who we called Lil Danny.

We had gone to Arizona with our son Robert. He had just been married on July 2, 2016. It was a lovely celebration. The colors were black and gold, and his beautiful bride wore white. Both sides of the family were present. They are a lovely couple who had a lovely wedding. After that, however, everything that was lovely turned into everything that was horrible.

I Had Gotten Stuck

Allow me start from the beginning

CHAPTER 1

You Breathed Life

It was 1975. As I was walking home from school, I heard this man's voice coming from the sky, saying, "Hey, beautiful Black girl, can I walk you home?"

Now I knew the Lord was in the sky, and I knew He loved me, but I couldn't believe He had come down to earth just to walk me home. I kept walking, but I started walking faster.

I heard the voice again. "Hey, beautiful Black girl, can I walk you home?" I was afraid to look up because the old folks used to say when you see the Lord face-to-face that means you have died and gone to heaven. I wasn't ready to die, so I wouldn't look up.

The next day as I was walking home from school, the same voice said the same thing: "Hey, beautiful Black girl, can I walk you home?"

I said to myself, *Don't look up, Rolinda, or you will die!* I kept walking.

Again, I heard, "Hey, beautiful Black girl, can I walk you home?"
This time something in me said, *Look up!*

I decided if I was going to die, I might as well die with the Lord walking me home. I looked up and sitting in the tree was Danny Golden, that boy from Edison High School who nobody could stand because he ranked (talked about) everybody.

I said, "Ugh, no! You can't walk me home!" and I took off running.

All that night, I thought about Danny Golden. He had called me beautiful, and he had wanted to walk me home. I was stuck on Danny Golden just that fast because he called me beautiful.

During my entire childhood, I can't remember anyone calling me beautiful. I was called fat, baldheaded, ugly, black, misbuilt, gap tooth, and then some, but never beautiful. *You're ugly. You're fat. You're baldheaded. You're black as midnight. You have ugly teeth; why is your gap so big?* I had started to believe the negative words said to me.

Danny Golden spoke life to me. He had deposited life into my spirit and soul. It was the first time anyone said encouraging, uplifting, or positive words to me, and I felt nervous, happy, uplifted, cheerful, and selfish. I say selfish because I took those words and hid them within my heart before he figured out, he made a mistake and wanted to take those words back.

I could tell Danny Golden wasn't like that. He meant every word he said, and he wasn't taking any of them back. I said to myself, *this boy sees something in me that no one else has ever seen. This boy doesn't even know me, and he called me beautiful; just imagine what he will call me once he gets to know me.*

The next day, I took a little more time to get dressed for school because I wanted to look extra cute for Danny Golden. I wanted him to notice me so he would call me beautiful again. I knew Danny would be waiting in the tree to ask if he could walk me home, and this time I was going to let him. After school,

I hurried to that tree just to hear those sweet words. As I got closer to the tree, I heard nothing. I thought, *Wait, is this the same tree?* Yes, it was the same tree, but Danny Golden was not there. It was a Friday, so I wasn't going to walk by that tree again until Monday. I was stuck all weekend. No one could imagine the horrible pain I was going through. Finally, someone liked me, someone thought I was beautiful, someone really showed me some attention, someone cared about me, Rolinda, but what did I do? I let him get away.

The entire weekend I stayed in my room, which I shared with my two sisters Vita and Jody. They would come in the room, acting like they needed something just to see if I was crying so they could go tell Mama. I didn't care. I was just hoping I hadn't lost the only boy who liked me, the only boy who spoke life into me, the only boy who I wanted to be with.

That was funny. I didn't even know him personally. I just knew what people said about him, but at that point I didn't care what people said. He'd called me beautiful and wanted to walk me home, so he was all right with me.

Sometimes when we listen to other people's opinions or perspectives of a person, we lose out on the blessing that awaits us. I was scared of Danny Golden because people said he ranked on everybody, but he didn't rank on me; he complimented me.

I was hoping and praying I didn't mess that up.

It was Monday morning. After school, I was just going to walk home as usual because I didn't want to be disappointed if Danny Golden wasn't up in that tree. As I approached that famous tree, I didn't look up because I didn't want it to seem too obvious that I was looking for Danny. I just passed right under it, looking down.

I didn't hear Danny, so I was kind of sad and disappointed. I thought I had missed the opportunity of letting him walk me home. As I passed the tree, I heard, "Hey, beautiful Black girl, can I walk you home?"

Yes, it was Danny Golden standing behind the tree. He wasn't in the tree this time; he was on the ground standing behind the tree. He said it again. "Hey, beautiful Black girl, can I walk you home?"

My heart started pumping to a different kind of beat, my hands became all sweaty, my eyes filled up with water because I was so happy, and my feet were stuck in place. I couldn't move. I was hypnotized and mesmerized. I was stuck on Danny Golden's voice. I was the happiest girl in the world because that boy nobody could stand had asked to walk me home. I was honored and ready.

I smiled and my gap-toothed smile and said, "No, you can't walk me home!" Where did that come from? I had waited for this moment and I had said no.

I started walking, but not too fast. I wanted Danny to catch me. He caught up to me and just smiled.

He grabbed my hand and said, "I'm walking my girl home!"

I said, "How you gone grab my hand and call me your girl! I don't know you, and I don't like you!" I shouldn't have said these things, because he could have just said "okay" and walked away.

He didn't; he replied, "Girl, stop all that fussing. You know you like me, and you're my girl!"

That was the beginning of Danny and Rolinda.

INSPIRATION

You Breathed Life in Me

I was just a young girl, fat and Black, is what they said.
Just a lonely little girl, ugly, and baldhead.
I was walking through life a misfit and unknown,
Trying to live my life sad and all alone.
No one knew the pain I was going through,
The loneliness, the suffering, my insecurity too.
I was fourteen years old with no love and no friend.
I didn't care if my life came to an end.
I was a sad, lonely girl, and a depressed one too.
I was miserable, but no one really knew.
I was ashamed of me and hated my looks,
But some special kind words were all it took.

The day I heard, "Hey, beautiful Black girl,"
It changed my entire life completely.
That boy Danny Golden had breathed life in me.

CHAPTER 2

Stuck on Words

Danny and I became inseparable. When you saw Danny, you saw me, and when you saw me, you saw Danny. I wouldn't go anywhere without Danny. He made me feel good. He made me believe that I was the prettiest girl in the world. Knowing that he chose me to be his girl made me feel that much more special.

Whenever I went out without Danny, my feelings would end up being hurt, and I would go home crying. The enemy knew how to get to me, how to hurt me, because all he had to do was use people and their words to bring up my past—the past that God had delivered me from when he sent Danny.

"Rolinda, you're still fat I see!"

"Have you gotten blacker?"

"I see you haven't had that gap fixed yet!"

"Your hair hasn't grown I see."

These words stuck with me and hurt me, and they were words Danny would never say.

Danny would come over to my house—well, it was my mama's house because I still lived at home, but I kept it clean. Anyway, he would come over, and I would be in my room crying because I had allowed the enemy to get to me with words. When I would come out of the room, Danny would just smile and say, "There's my beautiful Black queen." I had become Danny's queen. The crying and sadness left just that fast because now I was a queen.

It didn't matter to Danny where I lived, how I was raised, what kind of clothes I wore, how short my hair was, how fat I was, or how big my gap was. He only saw the beauty within me, and that made my life different.

Danny had a special way of making me feel like nothing in the world could hurt me, nothing could make me sad, nothing could make me unhappy, and nothing bad anyone said about me mattered. As long as I was with Danny, I was good. Danny became my escape from the cruel and ugly world. When I was with Danny, everything seemed like paradise, and everything was beautiful. No matter where he took me, it was beautiful just because I was with Danny and he made me happy.

Living in paradise with Danny Golden was the best feeling I have ever felt. He was truly an angel sent, my knight in shining armor, and the only best friend I had.

God knew exactly what I needed before I knew what I needed. Yes, I was young, but I knew the Lord for myself. I used to go over my grandma's—the late great Jonny Mae Ricks—house and sit at her feet while she told me stories of herself and the Lord. There were times when I would sit by her feet crying and all she would say was, "Rolinda, just keep your hands in the Master's hand." That's all she would say and nothing more. This taught me that no matter what I was going through, I could always trust God to see me through it. I knew one day I would be happy, but I could have never imagined it would be with Danny Golden, the boy no one could stand.

Danny would meet me after school and take me home. He had a white Chevy lowrider car; every time he picked me up felt like my prince charming had arrived to take his queen to her palace. It was just the projects, but Danny made me feel like a queen who lived in a palace.

Danny was seventeen at the time and worked for the City of Fresno. That is why he was up in that tree: he was pruning branches. I had myself a working man. Every payday, he would take my sisters and me to dinner, or he would say, "Tell your mom she doesn't have to cook. I'm going to bring some pizza over."

Danny would bring three or five large pizzas and we would all sit around the table smiling and looking at Danny. Everybody loved Danny, and everybody was happy to see me happy.

Danny made everyone happy, especially when we had friends over. Danny would rank on all of them; some laughed, some became upset, some tried to rank back, and some got up and went home. No one could out-rank Danny. My brothers' friends would come from all over just to rank battle with Danny, but no one out-ranked him. Danny owned the title of best ranker in Fresno.

Even though Danny ranked on everybody, he never ranked on me. He also didn't allow anyone else to rank or talk bad about me. He protected my feelings.

One day when Danny came over to visit, I had been crying again. He said, "Every time I'm not around you it seems like you're not happy, or someone has hurt you. As soon as you graduate, I'm taking you with me and no one will ever hurt you again."

In June 1979, I graduated, and by the end of that year, I had moved out of my mama's house and into my own apartment with

Danny Golden. It was our first apartment, our first time being on our own, and our first time living together as a couple.

Our son Danny Jr. was born on November 23, 1979. We called him Lil Danny, and Danny Sr. was now called Big Danny. We were the proud parents of a baby boy, and I thought our life was complete. It wasn't.

On March 25, 1984—my birthday—I asked Big Danny when we were going to get married. He looked at me and said, "Whenever you're ready." I started planning our wedding and on November 3, 1984, we were married in his mother's house.

Now we were complete in our relationship. We were married, we had a son, we had our own place, and we were complete. I had never felt this good in my entire life. I never imagined I would be as happy as I was married to Big Danny. He completed me, he loved me, he respected me, he protected me, and he appreciated me.

I was stuck on him, his words, his love, and his companionship.

INSPIRATION

I'm Your Woman and You're my Man

I met you back when I was young,
So immature but lots of fun.
The Lord put us together and closed the door.
You were mine and I was yours.

We grew together while making mistakes.
We forgave one another for goodness sake.
We were joined in marriage, which was good,
To live in righteousness like we should

We made a commitment when we said, "I do."
You hold onto me and I'll hold onto you.
I'm going to please you for the rest of my life
Because you're my husband and I'm your wife.
You entered my life when I needed a friend.
I became your woman and you became my man.
You shielded and protected the inner me.
My beauty and self-worth you helped me see.
I love you Big Danny because you first loved me.
Until death do us part, that's how it will be.

CHAPTER 3

My Man

Danny and I had become one. We were now raising three sons: Danny Jr., Martell, and Robert. My family was my world. I was the happiest woman alive. We were complete, I thought.

Our family loved the Lord. We had Bible studies and prayer meetings in our home with our sons. We were truly a family that prayed together and stayed together. I was baptized when I was a very young girl, but Big Danny had never been. One day he asked if I would be baptized with him and I said yes. We both went down in the water the same day, and we were complete.

I went everywhere with Big Danny. When I went places without him, the enemy would try to bring up my past by using people to say mean words to me. I would not cry; I would go home and tell Big Danny. Big Danny would say, "Babe, we love you here in this house. You don't have to go out looking for love anymore; you have it right here in this house."

He said nobody in that house would ever talk about me, make

me cry, or hurt my feelings. "If anybody in this house ever tried to hurt you," he said, "they will have to answer to me!" From that day forward, I stopped hanging out with people who made jokes about me, used me as a punch line, or who never had a compliment for me. Every time I was around those people, including family, loved ones, or friends, I felt unwelcome. I started hanging out with Big Danny and my boys.

Big Danny loved to barbeque, so every weekend he would throw some meat on the grill and tell me to invite my sisters. He loved my sisters because they loved and respected him. Big Danny became known as the Ranking Barbeque King. Everybody started coming over on the weekends because they knew the Goldens were cooking.

Everybody was stuck on my man.

Once our sons were all grown up, they moved out and started families of their own. Danny Jr. married Darlene, Martell married Latoya, and Robert married ShayShay. They all started building their own legacies.

It was just the two of us again; Rallo, our family dog, made three.

Our youngest son Robert made it to the NFL and played for the Pittsburgh Steelers. One Friday evening, Rob called and said, "Daddy, my coach wants to fly you and Mom out to meet y'all, because Saturday is family day."

Big Danny went into a panic; it was the first time I had ever seen Big Danny scared. He said, "Babe, I'm not going!"

"Big Danny, our son is counting on us to be there; you have to go, babe."

He said, "I can't get on no plane. I can't do it!"

"Yes you can, baby, yes you can."

That morning, I saw the look in Big Danny's eyes; he was terrified. We prayed and got on that plane. He kept his eyes closed while squeezing my hand the entire way. Big Danny was terrified, but he got on that plane for our son.

For the other games, he would just say, "Babe, take one of your sisters with you. I'll buy the ticket." This is how I started traveling with my sisters. Big Danny did not want to fly, and he did not want me to fly alone, so he paid for one of my sisters to go each time. I really enjoyed going to the games and meeting all of the players, their wives, and families. It was a very exciting time of my life.

My son called his dad every night after his football practice, and every evening after his game. He loved talking to his dad about football and his dad looked forward to their talks every evening.

Big Danny made every game that we were able to drive to: Arizona games, Oakland games, and even Los Angeles games, but when we had to fly, it was me and one of my sisters.

Big Danny was a proud dad, he would always say, "Babe, we have some good sons. They carry the Golden name well. We done good, babe."

All I would say was, "Yes we did, baby, yes we did."

INSPIRATION

A Family Is

A family is supposed to be close,
As close as we can be—
A bond that's held together
That's shared between you and me.
A family is shelter
When standing in the rain.
A family is loving,
Should never cause you pain.
A family is forgiving
Whatever happened in the past.
A family is forever—
Now you know that's supposed to last.
A family is protection
From all danger and its harm.
A family is security
When wrapped in Jesus's arms.
A family is a light
When walking in the night.
A family is to be cherished
So hold them close and hold them tight.

CHAPTER 4

The Wedding

It was July 2, 2016 and our baby son Robert had just gotten married. He was living in Arizona, but he was married here in Fresno. Rob and his beautiful wife ShayShay stayed in Fresno overnight because his dad wanted to host a big barbeque dinner for their reception while all of our families were still in Fresno.

It was a grand celebration. Both families were in our backyard celebrating, laughing, and enjoying one another. Big Danny knew he could barbeque. He just knew he was the barbeque king.

But something was different about Big Danny, he just sat in a corner very quiet all night. Usually he's the life of the party but not this time he was quiet, I just thought he was tired.

The next morning, on the fourth, we rode with Rob and his new wife to their home in Arizona. Big Danny had taken his two-week vacation, so we were going to spend one week in Arizona and one week at home resting.

We enjoyed our stay in Arizona. When it was time to go home, our son said he was sending us home on an airplane because he didn't want us to drive back. I saw that look in Big Danny's eyes again, but he knew we had to get home, so he said okay. This time, the airplane ride was different. Big Danny wasn't panicking; he was calm and peaceful. I couldn't put my finger on it, but it was good to see him relaxed.

As we boarded the plane, Big Danny said, "Babe, I want to sit by the window." *What*? That was a surprise. Before he didn't even want to sit on the plane, but now he wanted to sit by the window. I said okay.

As we were taking off, I saw him glance out the window, then close his eyes. About thirty minutes into the trip, he raised the shade, looked out the window, and said, "Babe, this is as close to heaven as I'm going to get."

I couldn't believe he was looking out the window. I said, "No, babe, you're going to make it to heaven because you're the best man in the world. You're a good husband, a loving father, a great companion, and everybody loves you, but most importantly, you accepted the Lord as your personal savior."

He smiled and held my hand. Then leaned over, kissed me, and said, "I love you Rolinda Golden."

"I love you too Big Danny." Just then, the spirit of the Lord whispered, "This is his last plane ride." I understood that to mean Big Danny was not going to fly again.

After we returned home, Big Danny lay down and rested. If anything needed to be done, he would say, "I'll get to it later. I'm going to just rest." That entire week, he rested peacefully without a care in the world.

That Thursday night, my sister was giving a birthday party and I asked Big Danny if he wanted to go. He said, "No, and I don't want you to go. I just want you to stay home with me." That is exactly what I did. We stayed home watching movies and cuddling up with each other.

I felt the peace of God all over Big Danny. It was like he didn't care about anything as long as we were together. He said it again: "I love you Rolinda Golden."

"I love you too Big Danny." He held my hand all night while laying his head in my lap.

We stayed up talking for a while, then Big Danny said, "You know, babe, I'm going to retire from work. I'm going to go in Monday and say I retire."

I said, "All right, now we will be able to be travel and won't have to hurry back because you have to go to work."

He said, "Yes, I'm going to retire. I have made up my mind."

My Mind Is Made Up

My mind is made up; it's time to retire.
I don't care about that job; they can just rehire.
I'm calling it quits; I want to be by your side.
I going to make sure no one ever makes you cry.
I'm going to retire as soon as Monday gets here.
I love you Rolinda, my queen, my dear.
You're someone special; I adore you so.
You make me happy; I hope you know.
The two of us have now become one;
Living life together is so much fun.
Yes, I'm going to retire as soon as Monday comes.
I glad the Lord told me
Rolinda is the one

I love you Rolinda,
Big Danny

CHAPTER 5

I Had Gotten Stuck

It was July 15, 2016. I had gotten up early because Big Danny asked me to fix him a big breakfast, so I said okay. I fixed bacon, sausage, chicken wings, hash browns, eggs, biscuits, and gravy with a glass of orange juice. Big Danny sat at the table and ate his breakfast. He would usually eat in his rocking chair, but this time he said, "I'll eat at the table, babe."

After breakfast, he sat in his rocking chair, looking at me and smiling.

I said, "What's wrong with you?"

He said, "That was the best breakfast ever."

"Well thank you, Big Danny," I responded.

Big Danny was rocking in his chair when he said, "I'm ready."

I replied, "Ready for what?"

He said it again: "I'm ready."

Again I said, "Ready for what?" He wouldn't answer me, so I said, "Okay, you're not talking to me."

I got up and walked to the back window because Rallo, our

family dog, was scratching at the window, wanting to come inside. I yelled out, "Rallo. Down!"

Big Danny said it again: "I'm ready." Then he got out of his chair and walked over to me at the window. He hugged me around my waist and said, "I love you Rolinda Golden."

I said, "I love you too, babe."

Then he said, "I'm going to lay down and take a nap. Wake me up in about an hour."

I said, "Okay, babe."

He kissed me on my neck and said it again—"I love you Rolinda Golden"—and walked to the bedroom.

My sister Faye had stopped by to visit and we talked for about an hour. I said, "Faye, I have to go wake Big Danny up. He wanted me to wake him up in an hour."

She said, "Okay, sis, I'll talk to you later."

I walked to the room and opened the door. Big Danny was stretched out on the bed with his eyes open. I said, "It's time to get up, Big Danny." He didn't respond. I said it again: "Big Danny, it's time to get up." Again, there was no response, so I walked over to him and went to shake him. As I laid my hands on his body, he was cold as ice.

I Had Gotten Stuck

I didn't know what to do or how to do it. I couldn't move so I just screamed, "Big Danny, don't leave me! Please don't leave me." It was too late; he was gone. I called 911. The operator was asking me so many questions and telling me to do all sorts of things, but it was too late. Big Danny was gone. His eyes were grey, and his body was cold.

My companion for forty-one years, the love of my life, my earthly protector, my husband, had just passed away.

Now it all makes sense to me: why he was so peaceful, why he was telling me he loved me, why he didn't want to do anything, why he wanted me to stay beside him, and the spirit of the Lord saying this was his last ride. It makes sense that Rallo wanted to come in the house so badly, and why Big Danny kept saying he was ready.

He made his peace with the Lord and he made sure I knew he loved me. He was ready, but I wasn't ready for him to go.

I Had Gotten Stuck

When the ambulance arrived, they tried working on Big Danny for about thirty minutes before they loaded him onto the gurney. In the meantime, Rallo was going crazy and trying his best to get into the house. Now I know why; Rallo sensed something was wrong and he wanted to come inside.

We all rushed to the hospital, hoping for a miracle to happen. My family was there along with some of Big Danny's family, my friends, Big Danny's friends, his coworkers, and my pastor.

While sitting in the waiting room talking and praying, I said a few words of encouragement to my family, which helped for the moment.

Finally, the doctor came out and said I could go to where Big Danny was. When I walked in, I saw about eight doctors and nurses around Big Danny. One was standing on the gurney that Big Danny was lying on, giving Big Danny electrical shocks. He was working hard trying to bring Big Danny back. One doctor said, "We've been working on him since he came in, but we cannot find a pulse."

There lay my knight in shining armor, my everything, my best friend, my sons' father, lifeless.

I said to the doctor, "Please let him be. He's gone."

I kissed him one last time and whispered in his ear, "Thank you for loving me the way you did. Thank you for breathing life in me."

I wished I could have breathed life back into him, like he had done for me, but I couldn't. I just held his hand and whispered in his ear. This made me numb; I was stuck, and I couldn't move.

The doctor took me by my arm and asked if he could walk me back into the family room. I said yes, but as I was walking away from Big Danny, I felt my legs giving out and my heart beating so fast it felt like it was about to leave my chest. The room was spinning, and I was sweating. I felt scared! I was scared to walk back into the world without Big Danny.

Everything I went through as a young girl creeped back in my mind, being talked about, being bullied, being lonely and being sad all this was trying to take ownership in my mind.

What was I going to do now?

As soon as I walked into the family room, I collapsed. I heard the doctor calling for help, I heard my mama say my name, I heard a lot of commotion, but I was stuck, and I couldn't respond.

Finally, after a few minutes, I was able to stand up. The doctor wanted to take me back to one of the rooms and evaluate me, but I said no. I just wanted to go home.

I couldn't believe Big Danny was gone. Why did the Lord take away the only man who ever loved me? This was unbelievable. It wasn't real. I needed to wake up and wake up right away.

I went home and walked into my bedroom, and I saw Big Danny lying there, stretched out on the bed, lifeless. I closed the door and went to lay on my couch. That was my sleeping spot for the next ten months.

INSPIRATION

The Death of A Loved One

The death of a loved one is an unanswered question: Why?
Why did my husband have to die?
See, I may not ever know the answer to that question that I asked,
But there's someone who knows it all and believe me He knows what's best.
Maybe Big Danny was suffering with an illness I didn't know,
And once he made his peace with God,
He said, "I'm ready, I'm ready to go."
No more suffering, no more pain,
No more storms and no more rain,
No more tears and no more fear,
No more cries that No hears,
No more sleepless and stressful nights,
No more enemy he has to fight,
No more worry about tomorrow,
No more heartaches and no more sorrow.
So, I'm just going to wipe my tears and dry my eyes
For my beloved Big Danny is on the master's side.
I'll see him again one fine day.

In the name of our Lord and Savior Jesus Christ, I pray.

CHAPTER 6

I Lost It

Well, the homegoing for Big Danny was beautiful. He was laid to rest looking just as handsome as he did when he was alive. We dressed him in a black suit with a red tie and a red hat. Big Danny loved his hats; he had a hat matching every pair of shoes he owned.

The funeral home was packed with family, loved ones, and friends. We didn't have a public repast; we just had our families come over to our house. I had so much company there with me, it really hadn't hit me that Big Danny was actually gone.

It wasn't until a month later, as I was by myself, when it hit me: Big Danny was gone and was never coming back. I believe that was my breaking point. That was when I lost it. That was when I realized I was all alone. That was when I really became stuck.

I started going into a dark place; everything around me became dark. I stayed in the house with the curtains closed. I didn't turn on any lights and I didn't turn on the television. I lived in darkness. I didn't open my door or answer my phone. I didn't want any company. I didn't want to go outside, and I didn't want anyone inside.

The only people I allowed into my home were my sons, their wives, and their children, my sisters, my mom, and my grandchildren. Other than that, no one was allowed to enter.

I hated being around people because they would always say the same thing. I got tired of hearing it, so I started isolating myself.

That was the worst thing I could have done.

Days, weeks, and months went by. I was still crying, still isolated, and still in disbelief. I had become a different person. I didn't care about anything or anyone—I just wanted Big Danny back.

I had become mad, upset, frustrated, emotional, bitter, sorrowful, careless, rude, evil, moody, unsociable, cranky, snappy, cold, unresponsive, unmotivated, unfriendly, ungodly, and unapproachable. I was mad at God because He took my Big Danny.

When I say I was mad at God, He knew it! I didn't talk to God, I didn't read His word, I didn't wake up and say, Thank You. I didn't acknowledge God at all. The only thing I said to God was, "Why did you take Big Danny?" Why did you take the only person that really loved me? Why Lord, Why? Before God could respond I just said, I don't want to hear it!

Every time I tried to get out of the house and be around people, all I would hear was, "Are you still crying? Big Danny is gone; he's not coming back. It's time so move on" or "Big Danny is in a better place; he wouldn't want you unhappy."

Every time someone said those words to me, I cut that person off. I avoided him or her. I didn't care who it was or who said it— that person was cut out of my life. I didn't want to hear those old hand-me-down words our ancestors used to say to someone who was grieving. They didn't know what else to say so they just said the same thing generation after generation.

About a year had went by, and I decided to go back to church. As soon as I walked through the door, people surrounded me, saying how sorry they were, and how good of a guy Big Danny was, and that he's in a better place—here we go again with all these ancestor sayings! Why couldn't someone just say, "I'm praying for you sister Golden," or give me a hug without saying anything? Why the same old words from every other person?

No one cared to ask how I was doing, if I was okay, or if I needed anything. Because I was a widow, no one cared to ask me about me.

People were always telling me about Big Danny, how good of a man he was, and how much he loved me. I was with this man for forty-one years. I knew him better than anyone at the church, but they were trying to convince me that they knew him—so I walked out and never went back.

The worst thing people can do is to tell us about our deceased husbands. We know all about them and we don't need outsiders trying to tell us anything about them. This is what make us mad. The same people who had so much to say after he's gone never had anything to say when he was living. Now, they say he was a good man, but he was a good man when he was living!

Sometimes it's best to say nothing instead of trying to tell a widow about her deceased husband. When I snapped, people wanted to call me rude or mean. What they failed to realize was that I did not want to hear what they were saying.

People are so quick to say whatever's on their mind without thinking about your feelings. They are so quick to tell you things they heard other people say, instead of being original and just speaking what God would have them to say. Sometimes God will have you say, NOTHING!

I Lost It

I wasn't going anywhere; I wasn't doing anything except sitting in my house, crying every night on the floor in the dark.

During the day, I tried to move around, I tried to be normal, I tried to come into the light, but darkness had me bound. When night fell, I fell.

I would fall to the floor in agony, screaming Big Danny's name. This was the worst pain I had ever experienced. I made myself sick. This went on every night for another year. I was all alone, isolated in my house, by myself. I wasn't eating because I didn't want to. I didn't want to do anything. I just wanted to be with Big Danny.

I believed I died Friday, July 15, 2016 at 1:00 p.m. right along with Big Danny, but for some strange reason I was still living.

Over time, my body stayed numb, my spirit stayed bruised, my flesh hurt, my attitude was ugly, and my life was unexciting. I could not have cared less if I lived or if I died; I just wanted to be with Big Danny.

Who was going to hold my hand? Who was going to hug me during the night when I was scared? Who was going to make sure no one hurt me?

Who was going to take me on date nights? Who was going to fix things when they broke? Who was going to love me and tell me I was beautiful daily? Who was going to keep me company? Who?

INSPIRATION

Who?

Tell me who is going to hold my hand when I fall.
Who was going to answer the phone when I call?
Who's going to be by my side?
Who's going to wipe my tears when I cry?
Who's going to tell me they love and appreciate me?
Who's going to tell me I'm the only woman they see?
Who is going to open the door and help me get in?
Who am I going to call my Heaven-sent man?

Who?

Who will be there when I'm sad and blue?
I don't know—don't even have a clue.
Who will take me out to eat?
Who will tuck me in to sleep?
Who will tell me "I love you, dear?"
Who's going to whisper sweet things in my ear?
Who can I call in the late midnight?
Who can I say is my husband and I'm his wife?

Who?

Who would have known you would leave me alone?
Who would have known I wouldn't be able to call you on the phone?
Who would have known July 15 would be our last day together?
Who would have known that you would be gone—gone forever?
Who?

CHAPTER 7

———

He Comes Back

Sometimes I would dream of Big Danny. He would come to me and say, "Follow me, babe. It will be better." He would come again and say, "I'm happy up here. Come go with me." He came at night when I was crying my heart out in my depressed state. I was hurting badly. I just wanted to die. I didn't want to keep going.

I knew he was coming to get me to take me back to heaven with him, but I wasn't ready to go. I thought I was, but I wasn't.

See, when people lose their companions with whom they have shared their entire lives, it is hard to move on. People become stuck and want to give up because they cannot go on without their companions—but they keep fighting.

One day, I was crying and lying on the floor and Big Danny came walking up in a white suit, with a gold vest, gold tie, and gold shoes. He was handsome. He reached out his hand to me and I grabbed it. He said, "Come with me." I followed him. We started walking into this dark room, it was so dark I couldn't see anything,

But I held on to Big Danny's hand. We kept walking, then suddenly we walked into this room that was all white, like we had walked into the clouds. Big Danny turned to me and asked, "You ready?" I said yes.

We started climbing up some beautiful golden stairs, he was holding my hand the entire way.

I knew I was dying and going to heaven with him. I believe I had climbed about twenty stairs. I was smiling and so happy because I was going with Big Danny. Suddenly, I heard, "MAMA". Don't Go We Need You!" It was my son Robert's voice. I immediately let go of Big Danny's hand and said I can't go! He turned to me and said, "Go Back." I watched him as he continued climbing up those golden stairs. I watched him until he disappeared in the clouds—then I woke up.

I don't care what people say: "Oh Danny didn't come back to get you. It was just a dream" or "Once you die, you don't come back." I just want to say, "How do you know? Have you died and not come back?"

How can someone tell you what you saw or didn't see, when you're telling that person what you saw? Whether it was real or a dream, I know what I saw. People think that when you are grieving, you have somewhat lost your mind as well. You might have lost your companion, you may have lost your appetite, you may have lost some family, friends, or loved ones, you may have lost some weight, you may have lost the desire to move on, and you may have lost some hair, but you haven't lost your mind.

Sometimes the Lord will show those who are grieving visions and dreams to get their attention, to bring them back to the light. I don't know why He does what He does. All I know is when I said He showed me something, I didn't care who believed me; I knew what he showed me.

I know a few people who have shared with me that when their mothers died, their fathers became stuck. As soon as he told his family that their mother had come to get him, he passed. Another wife lost her husband and told her family that their dad came back to get her; within days, she passed away. Once they said their goodbyes, they passed away.

Please stop telling people what they didn't experience. Just because you didn't experience it doesn't mean they didn't.

Some people are so religious that if they didn't read it in the bible it's not real!

That's why I developed a relationship with my Lord and Savior, so when He needs to show me something I won't have to question if it's real or not!

People have different kinds of experiences dealing with the death of a loved one. If someone says his or her spouse came back to get the person, just say, "I'm glad you didn't go back with him/her because we need you here"

Danny was coming to me constantly until I talked to my Aunt Shug. I told her Danny keep coming to get me, so she told me the story of her late husband Uncle Pete. She said that Pete kept coming to get her, but she told him she wasn't going with him so he should stop coming! She said that's what I had to tell Danny when he came again: tell him that you're not going with him so stop coming.

Sure, enough Danny came again, but this time I said, "Danny, I love you but I'm not going with you so you can stop coming." He hasn't come back since then.

When you share your experience with certain people, they downplay it because they think you're incompetent because you're grieving. They try to convince you it didn't happen, but you know what is real. You're not crazy; you're just stuck.

Sometimes you can't share with people who haven't experienced what you are experiencing. Reach out to someone who has been through what you are going through; he or she will understand it better. Even when people refer you to a sister or brother in Christ, if that person has not lost a spouse, he or she will not understand your pain. I don't care how many degrees that person has.

When your spouse comes to get you, just say, "I'm not going!"

INSPIRATION

"Stop Saying That"

"Are you still crying?"

Yes, I am.
Forgive me sir. Forgive me ma'am.
I lost my husband of forty-one years,
So please forgive me if I still shed some tears.

"You know he is in a much better place."

No, he is not; I just visited his grave.
Don't tell me he's in a better place. Have you been there?
You don't know where he's at. Stop acting like you care.
Stop saying that because you don't know.
I hear those same words everywhere I go.

"He wants you to move on and to be happy again."
"Don't worry, my sister, God will send you another man."

Stop saying that because you don't know God's plan.
I'm not thinking about another man.
Stop saying those words you heard you ancestors say.
Do like my grandma did: only open your mouth to pray.
Those words or statements are not needed at the time.
Think before you speak. Stop saying whatever is on your mind.
Just text "I love you" or "I'm praying with you."
Just drop off some food or water—that's what you can do.
Just give us a hug or hold our hands.
Stop saying, "God will send you another man."
It's not another man we're thinking about—
It's about being in darkness and trying to come out.

CHAPTER 8

———

Darkness

Well, it had been two years and I had not been back to church. I was kind of mad and a little bit hurt. I thought since I had lost my husband, the church was supposed to rally around me with love and support. That's what it said in the Bible. James 1:27 tells us "to look after orphans and widows in their distress and to keep oneself from being polluted by the world." Well, I guess when you become a widow, that's just what you have become: a widow. You're not in distress; you just lost your husband.

I was still living in darkness. I didn't move around, didn't smile, and was always down and crying. When my sons came around, I put on this fake disguise like I was all right. I didn't want them to see me still hurting because I knew they would be hurt.

This went on for another year, until one day my son Robert said, "Mama, come go to church with me."

Robert still lived in Arizona, but every time he came down, he went to Celebration Church. I didn't want to go, but because he asked me, I went.

Now as soon as I walked through the door, I started crying like a baby. I don't know why. I think it was because my spirit was happy to be back in a church and fellowshipping.

The pastor preaching at the time was Pastor Cheri Hand, the wife of senior pastor Randy Hand. Her sermon was titled "You Are Not Alone." I cried through the entire sermon, saying, "Yes, I am."

After she finished preaching, they did the altar call. I wasn't going up there because I didn't know them, and they didn't know me. I felt that was a good thing.

As I was walking out the door, the spirit of the Lord said, "Go back." I turned around and there stood this lady with her arms stretched out, waiting for me. It seemed like I ran to her and just collapsed in her arms. All she kept saying was, "You're not alone."

After she prayed with me, she started ministering to me. She said, "Sister, I felt like you before I came here. I was so lost and in a deep depression because I had lost my husband." "Corina"

Now I knew this was the Lord's doing because He sent me to a lady who lost her husband too, and she was all right. She went on to say, "You see that lady sitting right there? "Elaine" She lost her husband as well. He died in his chair." I cried and told her how I lost my husband and all she said was, "I told you you're not alone.

We became friends. I had finally met ladies who felt the way I was feeling. I saw both of them working in the church helping other women to keep living, and I fell in love with this church.

I've been at my new church home for four years now and I love it. I have come out of my depression and I am active again.

Sometimes you have to change your surroundings to heal. Sometimes you have to travel to unknown territory to heal. Sometimes you have to leave a familiar place to heal. Sometimes you have to make a change in order to be changed.

God will send you to get the help you need, but you must be

willing to go. For two years, I didn't want to go anywhere. The Spirit of the Lord was saying go, but I wasn't ready.

I still have moments when I cry, but I don't get stuck anymore. I will shed a tear, but I will move on.

I was finally ready to let Big Danny go. I stopped holding on to him as if I was waiting on him to return. I finally told myself, "Rolinda, Danny is not coming back. He's gone."

See, you have to come to the conclusion that your spouse is gone and is not coming back on your own.

No matter how many times people told me that Danny wasn't coming back, I didn't hear them; I wasn't listening. I thought they were just being cruel and mean by saying that to me. I know now they were telling me the truth, but it still didn't matter because I wasn't ready to let go.

Finally, I snapped out of it. I became unstuck.

Once you get to that point, you are ready to move on. Not until you get tired of going in and out of darkness will you be ready.

The first step to healing and becoming unstuck is admitting that your husband or wife is gone, and he or she is not coming back. This will tell your mind to get a grip and come back to the light.

Still when holidays, anniversaries, or birthdays arrive, or certain songs come on, I might shed a tear, but I won't go back into that dark place.

I used to go into a depressed state and get stuck for day, weeks, and months. Now when those special days or events come around, I may or may not shed a tear. If I do, it's only for a minute or two then I'm back to being me.

I made a choice to live again. I decided I wanted to stay around to see my grandchildren all grown up and married with kids of their own.

INSPIRATION

I Want To Live

I made a choice. I want to live.

I want to receive all my blessings God has to give.

I want to wake up to see another day.

I thank You Lord for making a way.

I thank you Lord for keeping me in your perfect will.

I thank You Lord for I want to live.

I thank you Lord for how you brought me out.

I thank you for delivering me out of the darkness and drought.

Lord, I want to enjoy my life. I want to live.

Down on my knees I will kneel;

I will thank You each and every day

Every time I open my mouth to pray.

You saved me, Lord, and brought me out of the dark.

You told me to just hold on to Danny within my heart.

You told me to let him go and trust in You.

So that's exactly what I am going to do.

I'm unstuck, Lord; I can receive all the blessings you give.

I'm your daughter, Rolinda, and I want to live

CHAPTER 9

Unstuck to Live

See, I had to come out of denial and admit that my husband was gone and wasn't coming back. That was my first step to coming out of the dark. So many times, we want to hold on to our husband's belongings, their clothes, their shoes, their hats, their car, and so on. However, these are material things. The longer we hold on to material things, the longer we will remain stuck.

Hold on to the memories that you shared together.

I had to change my surroundings. I stopped being around people who didn't uplift, encourage, or comfort me. I started spending time with positive people who understood what I was going through. The enemy knows your surrounding better than you do. He will keep you bound and depressed because he knows what you're going to do, where you're going, and who you're going to do it with. He knows your surroundings. He will use people to make sure you stay down in the dark. He doesn't want to see you happy; he doesn't want you smiling again. He wants you to be depressed, isolated, and weak. Change your surroundings; this will change your life.

I stopped allowing people to tell me how I should feel, how I should act, or what I should be doing. They would say, "You need to stop crying," but I couldn't. "You need to get out the house and go somewhere," but I was stuck. "You need to stop visiting his grave because he's not there," but I wanted to.

People will try to tell you what you need to do because they think they know what you need to do when you are grieving. Do what you feel like doing. I stopped listening to people because I realized that they didn't know what was best for me; I didn't even know what was best for me.

Do what you feel like doing when you feel like doing it. I cried when I wanted to cry, I ate when I wanted to eat, I got dressed when I wanted to get dressed, and I went out when I wanted to go out. I started wanting to do things, so I started doing things. I slowly started getting myself back.

I stopped isolating myself. Every time I felt like I was about to get stuck, I called one of my sisters or close friends to come over just to have someone to talk to.

You will know when you are headed into a dark place, but before you get in it, call someone you can trust. I thank God I had sisters and close friends.

Pray. Even when I didn't feel like it, I prayed. Even when I was mad at God for taking Big Danny, I prayed. I didn't say a prayer like I do now; it was more like an "I'm mad at you" conversation. Prayer is the key and the answer.

You will lose a lot of people in your life while you are grieving—people who said they loved you while your husband was alive. Family, friends, and loved ones will abandon you because they can't stand to see you hurting. They don't know what to say to you or they just didn't care in the first place. Whatever their reason was for abandoning you, when you come out of the darkness and become strong again, *do not go get them!* Leave them where they left you.

My son Robert opened Golden Charter Academy, the first Environmental Stewardship Charter Academy in the nation. I started volunteering to keep me busy and to get out of the house. Now I'm a full-time contractor with employees of my own. I'm the manager of the cafeteria, and I make sure all my babies eat. This brings me joy; I have found my purpose and I'm walking in it. That was the final step to coming out of the darkness: finding my purpose. We all have a purpose here on this earth, a purpose that is greater than what we can think, ask, or imagine.

It has been six years now since Big Danny passed away, and out of those six years, it took me four years to get where I am today. I'm stronger, I'm wiser, I'm better, I'm Rolinda.

INSPIRATIONS

I Came Out

I came out of darkness; now I'm free.

I'm ready to live again; it's time to be me.

I released Big Danny from the bondage in my mind.

I told myself, "Just let him go. It's for the good," and it's time.

I drew closer to God; I stopped being mad.

I stopped being angry, depressed, and sad.

I stopped being lonely, upset, and blue.

I stopped being isolated, withdrawn, and all alone.

I started going outside. I started leaving my home

I started going to family functions and picnics in the park.

I was no longer living in isolation, living in the dark.

The Lord brought me out of the darkness and into the light.

No more cloudy days; everything is bright.

I came out; I beat the odds.

Now I know why they said, "Let go and Let God."

I let go of the pain and suffering I was living with.

I didn't let go and I didn't quit.

I'm praising God!—and yes, that's a shout.

I'm living again. I came out.

SUMMARY

The Lord sent Danny to speak life to me when I was lonely, sad, and felt all alone. He sent Danny to help me become the woman I am today. Danny taught me how to live and enjoy life, and to enjoy it to the fullest. The Lord lent me Danny for forty-one years. During those years, we had three handsome sons who are closer to me than I could have ever imagined.

Danny was my knight in shiny armor, my protector, my angel sent from heaven, my loving husband, my baby, and my best friend.

We loved each other until death did, we part.

Because of Danny, the enemy cannot bring up my past to hurt me with words.

The enemy can no longer make me believe what is not true because Danny helped me believe in myself, I am a Beautiful Black Girl, I am someone special, I am loved.

When the Lord sends you someone special, hold on to that person, because one day you will experience the death of a loved one.

The End to The Beginning

Printed in the United States
by Baker & Taylor Publisher Services